How to Write a Story

Bentz Plagemann

HOW TO WRITE A STORY

Lothrop, Lee & Shepard Co.: New York

The author wishes to express his sincere thanks to the publishers listed below for permitting him to use the following excerpts from their books:

On page 35, the excerpt from Chapter 1, *Charlotte's Web* by E. B. White. Copyright 1952 by E. B. White. Reprinted by permission of Harper & Row, Publishers, and of Hamish Hamilton Ltd., London.

On pages 36–38, the excerpts from *Lord of the Flies* by William Golding. Copyright 1954, 1955 by Coward-McCann, Inc. Reprinted by permission of Coward-McCann, Inc., and Faber and Faber Ltd.

On page 32, the excerpt from "Where Are You Going, Where Have You Been?" from *The Wheel of Love and Other Stories* by Joyce Carol Oates. Copyright 1966, 1970 by Joyce Carol Oates. Reprinted by permission of the Publisher, The Vanguard Press.

This book is dedicated to the beginning writer
whose work will one day be known to the world.

Other books by Bentz Plagemann

Novels:

ALL FOR THE BEST
INTO THE LABYRINTH
THE STEEL COCOON
HALF THE FUN
THE HEART OF SILENCE

Novels about the Wallace family:

THIS IS GOGGLE
FATHER TO THE MAN
THE BEST IS YET TO BE
A WORLD OF DIFFERENCE

Books of non-fiction:

MY PLACE TO STAND
THIS HAPPY PLACE

Contents

:one:
Writing a Story

It is probably best to begin this book by saying that no one can really teach anyone else how to write a story. The writing of a story is an act of creation. This creative act has its beginning within the writer, and no one but the writer can bring about this initial impulse.

However, there is much that can be learned from the experience of others to help you write effectively. If you feel you have writing ability and long to try writing a story, you will not have to be taught to do this. But, as many would-be writers have found, it is not always easy to get your story down on paper so that it has the same impact you thought it did when you conceived it.

There is no magic formula for the writing of a story, and there are no arbitrary rules. But there are techniques that can be learned, and a knowledge of the basic techniques of writing can mean the difference between failure and success.

The purpose of this book is to give you an awareness of the techniques that make the craft of writing, and an inkling of the creative process that makes the art of writing. Because the act of writing begins with an idea, we must consider the creative process first.

Ideally, a story should come into being spontaneously. The idea for a story may come from some experience that you have. Or it may come from an episode in which others take part—friends, or members of your family, who then become the characters in your story. The story may come to you complete, with a beginning, a middle, and an end. Or it may come as a fragment of the final whole.

Once you have the idea for your story, you are most apt to be successful in getting it down on paper if the initial steps are taken quickly, with a kind of faith. Even though you may not be quite certain how it will come out in the end, you should go ahead fearlessly, using the exhilaration of your excitement and confidence to give you the momentum you need to carry it through to a conclusion.

Some writers have been known to compare the writing of this first draft of a story to skating over thin ice. One must not hesitate or look back, but proceed swiftly, if one is to reach the opposite shore. The reason for this is that it is all too easy to get bogged down in details if one attempts to polish the writing as one goes along. The object is to get the story down while it is fresh in your mind and you are still excited about it. Rewriting can be done later.

As you write, ideas and associations will well up from your subconscious mind. There you have stored, as in a computer bank, the memory of all that has happened to you and all that you have observed, even though a great deal of it is no longer retained by your conscious mind.

When a writer sits down to write a story he must allow his subconscious mind to open. This process, when observed by others, is usually referred to as "daydreaming." Much of a writer's time is spent alone in a room, lost in this sort of reverie. As he writes a story he will find that he falls ever more deeply into a state of concentration, so that he will become unaware of his surroundings or of any distractions. Almost without knowing he is doing it, he will draw on his hidden store of past experience and observation to explain or illuminate the episodes and characters in the story he is writing.

If the story goes well, a sense of urgency will replace the reverie of the daydream. As the characters take over and begin to live lives of their own, it will sometimes seem to the writer almost as if the story were writing itself.

At such a time it is not necessary to remember any rules. To write with rules in mind at this moment would merely be to place unnecessary obstacles in your path.

During this initial period of writing it is important also to find for yourself the actual physical method of writing that is most comfortable for you. Some writers train themselves to use a typewriter. Others prefer to write with a pencil. Some feel more comfortable with a pen. If it is the goal of the writer to master his tools so well that the reader will scarcely be aware of the words he is reading, then the writer must find for himself the physical method of writing that will best allow him to forget that he is actually writing. Scenes and images must be transferred to paper almost without his awareness of how he is doing it.

This writing of the first draft of a story is the most exciting and rewarding experience a writer has. Tests have shown that in the initial act of creating a story, a writer may easily expend as much energy as a construction worker on the job.

The first draft of a story, which may be written at one sitting or may require days or even weeks to complete, is the raw material from which your finished story will emerge. Later it will have to be shaped and polished, perhaps rewritten several times. But with experience you will learn that the finished version of a story will contain only as much suspense and passion as you have managed to put into the first draft.

Some writers like to make an outline of the plot before they begin to write the story. If you are able to do this you may find it helpful as a guide, even if you do not follow the outline but alter it as you go along.

Many writers feel that an outline is too restrictive, and do not like to write from one. They prefer to carry the elements of the story around in their mind and let the ideas grow and develop there while they are writing. It has been said that one of the attributes of genius is the ability to carry around a complicated or unresolved thought or problem in one's head for a very long time until a solution presents itself. It was by just such a process that Albert Einstein arrived at his theory of relativity. Leo Tolstoy's long and complex novel *War and Peace* took shape in his mind in the same way.

Every writer must practice this kind of sustained thought while his story is evolving in his mind.

:two:
How a Story Takes Form

Once the idea for a story has come to you and you want to start putting it down on paper, how do you begin? A fairy tale might conveniently begin with this sentence: "Once upon a time there was a beautiful princess who lived in a castle." Immediately the reader is given the basic information of who, when, and where.

This is all right for a fairy tale, where one castle or one princess is very much like another, but a story about real life must have at its beginning a greater sense of reality. When a story opens much will already have happened offstage in the lives of the characters. How do you let the reader know the necessary background of the characters so that you can go on from there?

The dramatists of ancient Greece solved this problem in the theater by inventing the prologue. Before the action of a play began, an actor representing a shepherd or a watchman or a guard, or even several actors constituting a chorus, would come out on the stage and tell or sing or recite what had happened to the characters up to the point at which the play would begin.

That cannot be done with a story. You cannot ask your readers to wait while you explain what happened to your characters in the past. Instead, it must all be done as a part of the story. You must manage to convey, at the very beginning, not only something of what has gone on before, but also a sugggestion of what is to come. At the same time you must explain who the characters are, where they are, and when the action is taking place.

O. Henry, who is regarded as one of the finest American writers of the short story, began *The Ransom of Red Chief* like this:

> It looked like a good thing: but wait till I tell you. We were down south, in Alabama—Bill Driscoll and myself—when this kidnapping idea struck us. It was, as Bill afterward expressed it, "during a moment of temporary mental apparition," but we didn't find that out until later.

In this example the information needed at the beginning of a story has been supplied. We know who the characters are, and we know where they are. Since we always assume that the time of a story is the present (the present time at which the story was written) unless the author tells us otherwise, we also know when it is happening.

We have been given some idea, too, of what went on before the story began. Obviously we are dealing with a couple of adventurers who are familiar with such things as kidnapping. We are not to take this too seriously, however; the expression "mental apparition" instead of "mental aberration" clearly shows that this is to be a funny story.

In writing your story you must keep in mind that no one will be forced to read it. The beginning of the story is your only chance to capture the attention of the reader and make him want to read on.

There are several ways of doing this. Some stories start with dialogue that piques our curiosity, some with a description of an interesting character we want to learn more about, some with a dramatic situation that makes us read on to discover how it comes out. Your opening lines should give some hint of the conflict, some suggestion of tension or suspense.

In the middle part of the story this conflict is developed. The characters play out the tension of this conflict against each other until it reaches a climax. At this point of climax something will happen to the characters, or in their lives, so that they will never be quite the same again. This episode in the story is called the "necessary scene," and it is so important to the success of the story that it will be dealt with in a separate chapter.

After this the story will head very quickly toward an ending that seems almost inevitable after the outcome of the climactic scene. The conflict of the story has been resolved, in one way or another.

The arrangement of the story is called the plot, and to have a plot you must have conflict. In a novel the conflict may take an abstract form. It may be between a character and his environment, those forces in his life over which he has little or no control, as in Dickens' novel *Oliver Twist*. Or the character may be a helpless victim of a government or political system, as in George Orwell's *1984* or the existentialist novels of Franz Kafka. The conflict may be between the ideals or principles the characters represent, as in Dostoevsky's *Crime and Punishment* and *The Brothers Karamazov*.

Unlike the novel, which has room for many characters, many episodes, and even many conflicts, the short story is concerned with but one conflict, sometimes within the character, but more generally between two people. These two people are technically known as the protagonist and the antagonist. The protagonist is the character who takes the leading part. The antagonist is the character in the story with whom he must contend.

Sometimes there is an actual object at stake in the conflict. In a spy story, for example, the conflict between the hero and the villain may be for the possession of secret plans, or the design of a new weapon, or microfilmed information. In a Western story the good guy struggles against the bad guy for land or for cattle, or for a mining claim. A love story may be about the hero and his rival for a girl.

Sometimes the stake is not an object. It could be honor, or glory, or revenge. A love story may be a conflict between a boy and the girl he hopes to win over against her early objections to him. The conflict may also be within ourselves, for often we find our worst enemy in our own inner nature, which must be overcome before we are able to find fulfillment in our lives.

Much of life is in the nature of a conflict, and if we look at it in this way, many examples come easily to mind. In our relationships with our teachers, our parents, our brothers and sisters; with the opposing members of an athletic team; with those with whom we must compete for a job, and with our eventual employer, the seeds of conflict are always present, and may provide us with the material for a story.

Often stories are concerned with conflicts of a modest dimension, based on a personal experience or that of a relative or friend. Let us say you are writing the following story: Tom quarrels with his parents and runs away from home. He is disillusioned by what happens to him after he runs away. He returns home.

There, in brief, is the outline for the story. There is its beginning, its middle, and its end. Also, in the quarrel Tom had with his parents we are supplied with a conflict. This is the cornerstone of your story. Upon that will rise the structure.

What happens to Tom while he is away is part of the story you have to imagine. After all, you as the author may not know what actually happened to him, or may have heard about it only secondhand after Tom returned. Perhaps you decide that instead of being disillusioned, Tom has an experience while he is away that enlightens him in some way. Instead of being merely chastened when he returns home, he may bring new insight, see his friends in a different light, and meet his parents on new ground, so that the conflict of the story will be resolved in a way that the reader will accept as a believable part of life.

Whatever you decide, this is the point at which you will actually be creating your story and bringing into being something that did not exist before.

It has been said many times, but it is worth repeating, that a writer must write about what he knows. Stories are about people, and the people you know best are your family and friends.

As a writer, you will hold a mirror up to life. In this mirror will be reflected your own image, the images of the people nearest you, and the background in which you have lived.

The work of a writer like Charles Dickens is an excellent example of this. *David Copperfield* is the story of the poverty and hardship of Dickens' own childhood. In *David Copperfield* all of the characters were based on people he knew, including his own father, who was the model for Mr. Micawber.

Mark Twain, whose real name was Samuel Clemens, is another writer whose life can be seen reflected in his stories. In *Tom Sawyer* and *Huckleberry Finn* he wrote about himself, his boyhood friends, and his family. People living today in Hannibal, Missouri, where Mark Twain was born and grew up, can show visitors the actual places where many scenes in these stories took place. If you go there, they will tell you about the people in real life from whom the characters in the stories were drawn.

Louisa May Alcott was another writer who drew upon her own experience for characters and plot. *Little Women* is the story of the life she and her sisters led in Concord, Massachusetts, at the time of the Civil War.

The images in the mirror that any writer holds up to life are of course distorted by his interpretation of what he sees there. A person may seem different to a teacher than he does to a close friend, while his family may see him another way entirely. Aside from this, it is necessary in writing a story to select the details you wish to use from the images in the mirror. It is at this point that creative writing becomes art, as distinct from journalism.

In writing a report for a newspaper, for example, all the details must be put down just as they were seen. But a story that is merely a mirror reflection of life would be lacking in any particular interest or excitement. Art is a process of the selection of details for the purpose of achieving a definite effect. The attitude of the writer toward the people or events of his story, as well as his selection of the details that will bring a semblance of reality to them, transforms the raw material of life into art and determines whether a story will be funny or tragic, ironical or romantic, or whatever category in which you may choose to write.

The writers we have just named—Dickens, Mark Twain, Louisa May Alcott—were masters in this art of arousing our emotions to respond to the materials they had selected from life.

:three:
The Characters of
Your Story

In one important definition, a story is said to be *character in action.* As the characters develop, they will seem to reveal new elements of their personalities that will cause them to react to one another differently from the way you had planned. They will begin to take on an existence of their own, and the story may grow and develop quite differently from the way you expected it would when you began.

Lillian Hellman, the playwright, has said that before she starts to write a play, she writes an imaginary biography of each of the characters in it. She must know what their childhood was like. She must know what their parents were like. She must know what their hopes and ambitions are, what their triumphs and disappointments were. She must know everything about them, right up until the moment the play begins. None of these imaginary biographies will be used in the play, but because she has so thoroughly understood the characters before she began to write, everything they do and say in the play will be in character.

In writing a story you must have the same goal. You must learn to know your characters so well that when they appear in a story they will be instantly credible and believable, and everything they do and say will be in character. Whether you write about an intimate friend, a member of your family, or someone met once at a party, there will be a lot of background imagining and making-up to do, for we are, all of us, in one sense or another, a mystery to others. We are closed to the world, in an effort to preserve our own privacy. No one is fully known to anyone else in real life, in the way that a character in a story must seem to be to the reader.

It is perhaps well to remember that the magic ingredient in all of this, if there is any magic ingredient, is yourself. A part of yourself will be in every character you create, for only in the way you react to things will you find understanding of the way others react.

In the actual writing of a story much of this musing and imagining and creating of background for a character will not be used, just as Lillian Hellman's make-believe biographies are not used in her plays. You would not want to burden your reader with all of this information, or delay the telling of the story with it. Yet, in some wonderful and mysterious way, all of this private knowledge you have of your characters will be in the pages of your story, between the lines, so to speak. As you gain in skill as a writer you will learn to brush in a character with swift and telling strokes, employing only the most meaningful, vivid details, which will, at the same time, express whole areas of understanding and knowledge of your characters.

A person who has aroused your interest or curiosity and prompted you to think of him as a character for a story may remind you of others you have seen or known, perhaps similar in nature. We do, all of us, even as individuals, share traits and mannerisms with others. We speak of a certain "type" of person. Musing on this person, in the reverie or daydream which is so much a part of writing, you may begin to see him as a prototype of others, and presently a new character will emerge, based on a real person, but larger than life. Your real-life model will have disappeared inside, and what the reader will see is a person unique and new.

Let us see how Charles Dickens accomplished this when he introduced Mr. Micawber in *David Copperfield:*

> The counting-house clock was at half-past twelve, and there was general preparation for going to dinner, when Mr. Quinion tapped at the counting-house window, and beckoned to me to go in. I went in, and found there a stoutish, middle-aged person, in a brown surtout and black tights and shoes, with no more hair upon his head (which was a large one, and very shining) than there is upon an egg, and with a very extensive face, which he turned full upon me. His clothes were shabby, but he had an imposing shirt-collar on. He carried a jaunty sort of stick, with a large pair of rusty tassels

to it; and a quizzing glass hung outside his coat—for orna-
ment, I afterward found, as he very seldom looked through
it, and couldn't see anything when he did.

"This," said Mr. Quinion, in allusion to myself, "is he."

"This," said the stranger, with a certain condescending roll
in his voice, and a certain indescribable air of doing something genteel, which impressed me very much, "is Master
Copperfield. I hope I see you well, sir?"

A writer must have a good eye, a candid way of looking at
people without personal bias, as Dickens has so ably dem-
onstrated here. He has skillfully selected just those details
that will bring the character to life. How would you go about
doing this if, for example, you met someone for the first time
who made such an impression upon you that you felt you
must use him in a story?

The circumstances under which you meet this person will
contribute to the building of his personality as a character.
If you met him at a friend's house, this circumstance will
tell you something about him, for you know your friend's taste
in friends. You will have observed how he was dressed, and
what this seems to indicate about his social background or
economic level. You will have observed his state of health, his
grooming, the condition of his shoes, the way he sat or stood.
Even with so little information as this, if he has roused your
writer's interest or curiosity you may steal him, so to speak,
and plant him in your mind, and begin to build a fictitious
personality around him.

To introduce him as a character, you may begin with an
observation of external details. You may tell the reader the
color of his eyes, his hair. You may mention his height. You

will almost certainly indicate whether or not he is physically attractive. As you practice your craft you will also learn that a character's manner of speaking and choice of words are very revealing. These details, superficial as they may seem, help to establish the character as a real person. We will explore this subject further in the chapter on dialogue.

:four:
The Point of View of
the Storyteller

Before you begin to write your story you must decide who is going to tell it. On thinking it over, you will begin to realize that a number of people could tell it, including any one of the characters themselves. Whatever decision you make, it must be final and consistent. It is important for the reader to know from the very beginning which character he is to identify with, and from what vantage point he will watch the story as it unfolds.

Basically, there are three points of view from which to write a story: the all-knowing, the first person, and the third

person. None of these is the "right" way or even the preferred
way to write a story. Each has advantages and disadvantages.

You may decide you want to write the story as if it were
being observed from above by someone who knew all about
the characters, past and present. This is the all-knowing point
of view in which the writer describes what happens almost
as if he were God—or as if he were a fly on the wall, seeing
and hearing everything, without taking any part in the story
or being noticed by those who do. This point of view is less
used today, perhaps because the movies and television have
amply supplied us with an impersonal view of life.

War and Peace by Leo Tolstoy, considered by many critics
to be the greatest novel ever written, was written from this
point of view, as were many other novels of the nineteenth
century. Here is a description from that book of Napoleon
and his army, engaged in their ill-fated attempt to try to con-
quer Russia. You will notice that the all-knowing point of
view and the all-seeing eye combine to give the impression
of a vast historical panorama unfolding on a wide movie
screen:

> Seeing, on the other side, some Cossacks and the wide-
> spreading steppes in the midst of which lay the holy city of
> Moscow, the capital of a realm such as the Scythia into which
> Alexander the Great had marched—Napoleon unexpectedly,
> and contrary alike to strategic and diplomatic considerations,
> ordered an advance, and next day his army began to cross
> the Nieman.
>
> Early in the morning of the twelfth of June he came out
> of his tent, which was pitched that day on the steep left bank
> of the Nieman, and looked through a spyglass at the streams

: 27 :

of his troops pouring out of the Vilkavissi forest and flowing over the three bridges thrown across the river. The troops, knowing of the Emperor's presence, were on the lookout for him, and when they caught sight of a figure in an overcoat and a cocked hat standing apart from his suite in front of his tent on the hill, they threw up their caps and shouted: *"Vive L'Empereur!"* and one after another poured in a ceaseless stream out of the vast forest that had concealed them and, separating, flowed on and on by the three bridges to the other side.

You can also use the all-knowing point of view in a more intimate way, to make the reader feel he is present in person at a scene. It was a favorite device of Charles Dickens. In his familiar story *A Christmas Carol*, this is how he described the family of Bob Cratchit as they prepared themselves for Christmas dinner:

> Then up rose Mrs. Cratchit, Cratchit's wife, dressed out but poorly in a twice-turned gown, but brave in ribbons, which are cheap and make a goodly show for sixpence; and she laid the cloth, assisted by Belinda, second of her daughters, also brave in ribbons; while a Master Cratchit plunged a fork into a saucepan of potatoes, and getting the corners of his monstrous shirt collar (Bob's private property, conferred upon his son and heir in honor of the day) into his mouth, rejoiced to find himself so gallantly attired, and yearned to show his linen in the fashionable parks. And now two smaller Cratchits, boy and girl, came tearing in, screaming that outside the baker's they had smelt the goose, and known it for their own; and basking in luxurious thoughts of sage-and-onion, the young Cratchits danced about the table, and exalted Master Peter Cratchit to the skies, while he (not proud, although his

collar nearly choked him) blew the fire, until the slow pota-
toes bubbling up, knocked loudly at the sauce-pan lid to be
let out and peeled.

It is important to remember when you write from this point
of view that you must let the characters reveal themselves
without betraying any attitude or opinion of your own. You
must make it seem as if the reader is observing the action as
it happens, without the obstacle of the personality of the
writer.

This is often hard to do. It is not always easy to keep your
own opinions out of a story. That is why writing from the
first-person, or "I" point of view, appeals to many authors.
Here the writer is in the foreground of the story at all times.
Because he is writing as if he were someone in the story, he
can freely express that character's opinions and judgments
about the other characters. Writing in the first person can be
a very satisfying experience.

One of the most famous lines in fiction illustrates the sense
of immediacy and the impact that can be created in writing
in the first person. It is the opening line from Herman Melville's *Moby Dick*, which goes, simply, "Call me Ishmael."
The first two sentences of the novel read like this:

> Call me Ishmael. Some years ago—never mind how long
> precisely—having little or no money in my purse, and nothing
> particular to interest me on shore, I thought I would sail
> about a little and see the watery part of the world.

At once the reader knows two things. Herman Melville may
be writing from his personal experience, but he is not writing

autobiography or memoir. He is writing a novel, and he has given himself a fictional character and a name, so that he can serve in a double capacity, both as narrator of the story and a character in it.

This is distinct from the manner Mark Twain so often employed in telling a story in the first person. When he wanted to tell an anecdote in which he did not take part as a character, he simply went ahead as himself. A good example is *The Celebrated Jumping Frog of Calaveras County,* which begins like this:

> In compliance with the request of a friend of mine, who wrote me from the East, I called on good-natured, garrulous old Simon Wheeler, and inquired after my friend's friend, Leonidas W. Smiley, as requested to do, and I hereunto append the result.

Here is Mark Twain himself telling a story, without any effort to disguise himself, and we know with pleasure that he will bring to it his special dry wit, his irony, and his sense of the ridiculous. He will make us see the characters of the story as he saw them, but he will not take part in the story.

A third option is open to you in writing a story from the first person point of view. You may prefer an even deeper involvement and place yourself entirely inside one character, who would not have perspective enough to see the story as a whole. You may even choose to be a person of another race or another color, or even a person of the opposite sex.

William Faulkner was a master at this form of writing. Here, in his novel *As I Lay Dying,* he speaks to us as a woman named Cora:

So I saved out the eggs and baked yesterday. The cakes turned out right well. We depend a lot on our chickens. They are good layers, what few we have left after the possums and such. Snakes, too, in the summer. A snake will break up a hen-house quicker than anything.

It is exciting and sometimes great fun to experiment with this form, as you can see. Putting yourself inside the mind of a friend or someone you have observed may bring you added insight into that person's character.

However, it is important to remember that writing in the first person has one disadvantage. With it, you may never describe anything the narrator does not actually see. You may not, for example, say, "Meanwhile, back at the ranch . . ." because the first-person narrator will have no way of knowing what is going on back at the ranch in his absence.

The third-person point of view is the form most commonly used today. The difference between it and the all-knowing point of view is that in the simple third person, you do not pretend to be all-knowing. You do not pretend to know the inner thoughts of all the characters. Instead, you choose one character. Through him you will tell your story, sometimes as if you were inside his head looking out, or sometimes as if you were merely looking over his shoulder, letting the reader know indirectly by his actions just what is going on in his thoughts.

Having done this you then, in effect, take one step backward, so that your central character can be seen in the larger context of your story. You can describe what goes on in the story around this character. You reserve your right of judgment, not only about this central character, but about the other characters as well. You can express how you feel about the other characters in the story through the thoughts or actions of this central character. This character can be anyone in the story. It can even be you, disguised in the third person under another name.

Here is the beginning of a story by Joyce Carol Oates, called *Where Are You Going, Where Have You Been?* It is an excellent example of the third-person point of view.

> Her name was Connie. She was fifteen and she had a quick nervous giggling habit of craning her neck to glance into mirrors, or checking other people's faces to make sure her own was all right. Her mother, who noticed everything and knew everything and who hadn't much reason any longer to look at her own face, always scolded Connie about it. "Stop gawking at yourself, who are you? You think you're so pretty?" she would say. Connie would raise her eyebrows at these familiar complaints and look right through her mother, into a shadowy vision of herself as she was right at that moment: she knew she was pretty and that was everything. Her mother had been pretty once, if you could believe those old snapshots in the album, but now her looks were gone and that was why she was always after Connie.

The third-person point of view may not have the scope and the drama of the all-knowing point of view. It may not have the intimacy and the impact of the first-person point of view. But it does have many advantages and much can be done with it.

With practice you will learn which point of view will serve you most effectively for any particular story you may want to write.

:five:
The Use of Conversation

No matter how clearly or vividly a character is described in a story, the reader will not really "see" him until he speaks. The speaking voice is, in some way, the signature of the personality.

The writer Somerset Maugham once said that whenever he found himself wondering if it could really be possible for each person on earth to be distinctly different from every other person on earth, he reminded himself of the snowflakes, of which no two are ever alike. Your speaking voice is the testimony of your individuality.

We all know how easy it is to recognize a friend on the telephone by the sound of his voice. How does a story writer go about making the reader hear the sound of the voices of his characters?

To begin with, along with a good eye for detail, a writer must have, or he must develop, a good ear for the way people talk, just as an actor or an actress in the theater must. Of course, in a play the actor has the advantage of his own voice to help in the portrayal of character, and he can assume or mimic an accent or intonation of voice. But a good part of the individuality of any person is revealed by his selection of words and by the way he uses them in conversation. And that is something that, as a writer, you can put down on paper. We all feel we know how Fagin sounded in *Oliver Twist,* or Holden Caulfield in *Catcher in the Rye,* even if we have never heard these characters portrayed by actors.

As a writer, you have one major and unexpected advantage working for you. If, in the writing of a story, you capture the interest of the reader at the very beginning, then a sort of unconscious collaboration develops between you and the reader. The reader is so anxious to get on with the story that he will actually help you. If you are able to strike the right note with the characters at the very beginning, if you have given them words to say that seem appropriate, then the reader himself will supply the tone of voice.

But it is important to repeat that it must be done in the story as quickly as possible, for until a character speaks he cannot really be seen.

In Edward Everett Hale's famous story "The Man Without a Country" there is a memorable example of the use of speech, although it is almost too long delayed for the success of the story. Today it takes patience to get into this story, but Edward Everett Hale wrote in a more leisurely day, when there were fewer demands on the reader's free time. He felt he could indulge himself, as the Greek dramatists did, with a prologue. The story begins slowly, with a description of the background of the story, of what went before. No character speaks for some time, but when, after several pages, the major character does speak, when, at his court-martial, he cries out in what the author describes as "a fit of frenzy" to the president of the court, saying, "Damn the United States! I wish I might never hear of the United States again!" we feel as if we have been seized by the back of the neck and thrown into the story. Then we are ready to follow, with a mounting sense of involvement, the long story of the tragic destiny of Lieutenant Philip Nolan.

By contrast you can see how effective it is to open at once with conversation. Here is the beginning of E. B. White's famous children's book, *Charlotte's Web*:

"Where's Papa going with that ax?" said Fern to her mother as they were setting the table for breakfast.

"Out to the hoghouse," replied Mrs. Arable. "Some pigs were born last night."

"I don't see why he needs an ax," continued Fern, who was only eight.

"Well," said her mother, "one of the pigs is a runt. It's very small and weak, and it will never amount to anything. So your father has decided to do away with it."

"Do *away* with it?" shrieked Fern. "You mean *kill* it? Just because it's smaller than the others?"

With the mention of the weapon of the ax in the first line, the reader is hooked. He reads on to find out whether Fern will be able to prevent the slaughter of the littlest pig, who of course is rescued and becomes the remarkable Wilbur.

You must be cautious, however, and know what you are doing, for one common error among beginning writers is to let one character or other characters speak too much at the beginning of a story. They sometimes feel they can explain something the reader should know by having one character tell it to another, even though it is something the other character already knows. Be on guard against this kind of contrived exposition.

On the other hand, beginning writers sometimes believe they can just *tell* the story. A certain amount of explanation may be necessary to a story, but a very important rule to remember in writing a story is: *Show, don't tell.* Show the action taking place, rather than tell about it after it has happened.

Learning to write a conversation is not so difficult. With a good ear and a little practice, the art of writing conversation can be mastered.

Here, as an example, is an exchange between two boys who are castaways on an island, in William Golding's *Lord of the Flies:*

"What's your name?"
"Ralph."
The fat boy waited to be asked his name in turn but this proffer of acquaintance was not made; the fair boy called

Ralph smiled vaguely, stood up, and began to make his way once more toward the lagoon. The fat boy hung steadily at his shoulder.

"I expect there's a lot more of us scattered about. You haven't seen any others, have you?"

Ralph shook his head and increased his speed. Then he tripped over a branch and came down with a crash.

The fat boy stood by him, breathing hard.

"My auntie told me not to run," he explained, "on account of my asthma."

"Ass-mar?"

"That's right. Can't catch me breath. I was the only boy in our school what had asthma," said the fat boy with a touch of pride. "And I've been wearing specs since I was three."

The author is using the practiced ear for the sound of speech that the writer must have or develop. By giving us the conversation of these boys, even so briefly, at the opening of the story, he gives us a sense of them at once. We feel that we know what they are like, and even hear and see them. Also, the story is in motion. The use of conversation as a device to move the story forward is a very important part of its function. The story is moving, and the characters are being developed even as we are introduced to them.

After an interruption, the conversation continues:

"I expect we'll want to know all their names," said the fat boy, "and make a list. We ought to have a meeting."

Ralph did not take the hint so the fat boy was forced to continue.

"I don't care what they call me," he said confidentially, "so long as they don't call me what they used to call me at school."

Ralph was faintly interested.

"What was that?"

The fat boy glanced over his shoulder, then leaned toward Ralph.

He whispered.

"They used to call me 'Piggy.'"

Ralph shrieked with laughter. He jumped up.

"Piggy! Piggy!"

"Ralph—please!"

Piggy clasped his hands in apprehension.

"I said I didn't want—"

"Piggy! Piggy!"

Ralph danced out into the hot air of the beach and then returned as a fighter-plane, with wings swept back, and machine-gunned Piggy.

"Sche-aa-ow!"

He dived in the sand at Piggy's feet and lay there laughing.

"Piggy!"

Piggy grinned reluctantly, pleased despite himself at even this much recognition.

"So long as you don't tell the others—"

Piggy, it is clear, is a natural-born victim.

With this example we see the characters, we have some sense of what they are like as people, the story is in motion, and we also hear emotion being expressed, which is another of the major functions of the use of conversation in a story. Emotion of all kinds may be expressed in conversation—fear, anger, joy, love.

It sometimes helps to read the conversation of your characters aloud after you have written it. Each character must be different from the other, and recognizable by means of his speech, which must be consistent with his characterization.

To sum up, one might say that the first purpose of dialogue in a story is to bring the characters to life. After that its use is to further the action of the story.

:six:
The Use of Description

Although description has more than one function in a story, its first purpose is to set the scene.

In the stories of Ernest Hemingway, many of which are written almost exclusively in terms of conversation between the characters, description frequently serves only this basic function—to let us know where the characters are.

When two characters speak in a room, it helps to have a description of that room, although it is not absolutely essential. Often the barest minimum of description, simply an indication of where the characters are, will do. After that the unconscious collaboration between the author and the reader will take over. Remember that the reader wants to know only those details that it is necessary for him to know; he does not want to be told too much. He does not want to be robbed of the pleasure of creating his own part of the story.

To illustrate this point, here is Jack London writing in *The Call of the Wild:*

> When Jack Thornton froze his feet in the previous December, his partners had made him comfortable and left him to get well, going on themselves up the river to get out a raft of saw-logs for Dawson. He was still limping slightly at the time he rescued Buck, but with the continued warm weather even the slight limp left him. And here, lying by the river through the long spring days, watching the running water, listening lazily to the songs of birds and the hum of nature, Buck slowly won back his strength.

In this example the author has used description as sparingly as salt. Without salt, food would lack much of its flavor but too much would ruin it. Description is necessary to a story, but its use is personal. It is your style. Style may well be a part of writing that cannot be taught. Let us say that style is what you are. The way you use language reveals your spirit and your personality. It is the way you look at things. Therefore the description in your story, or the absence of description, is a part of your style as a writer.

Description of any kind will never be neutral. It will always influence the reader in one way or another. As a writer, you must be certain that the mood you are creating is one you deliberately wish to create.

It is never possible for any of us to look at something with complete objectivity. The way a room or a scene looks to you may be very different from the way it looks to someone else. Teen-agers know all too well that their cheerful clutter of books and records and clothes carelessly dropped on the floor can affect a parent in a completely opposite way. And everyone knows how a room seems to change when a happy person comes into it, or how we are affected on a rainy day if we go into a gloomy room where there is insufficient lamplight.

It is also possible to try to describe scenes or happenings at greater length in an impartial way, so that the reader will feel that he is coming to his own conclusions without being influenced by the writer. This is an effective device in mystery stories, where often we feel that we are not getting any help at all from the writer but must wait until things work out by themselves.

Edgar Allan Poe knew well the effectiveness of such impartial description. He described a scene as if he were listing objects in a catalogue, and the seeming absence of any person behind the written words served to increase the sense of terror. In what are called his tales of mystery and horror he practiced this device with mastery. Here Poe sets the scene for the ball in his story "The Masque of the Red Death":

> The seventh apartment was closely shrouded in black velvet tapestries that hung all over the ceiling and down the walls, falling in heavy folds upon a carpet of the same mate-

rial and hue. But in this chamber only, the color of the windows failed to correspond with the decorations. The panes here were scarlet—a deep blood color. Now in no one room of the seven apartments was there any lamp or candelabrum, amid the profusion of golden ornaments that lay scattered to and fro or depended from the roof. There was no light of any kind emanating from lamp or candle within the suite of chambers. But in the corridors that followed the suite, there stood, opposite to each window, a heavy tripod, bearing a brazier of fire that projected its rays through the tinted glass and so glaringly illuminated the room. And thus were produced a multitude of gaudy and fantastic appearances. But in the western or black chamber the effect of the fire-light that streamed upon the dark hangings through the blood-tinted panes was ghastly in the extreme, and produced so wild a look upon the countenances of those who entered, that there were few of the company bold enough to set foot within its precincts at all.

In this scene Poe knew exactly what he was doing. He was using description to serve a specific purpose. As readers we are not aware of his presence in the story, but only of the effect he wished to produce.

This detachment is not easy to achieve, and it is not always desirable. Sometimes you may want your readers to know how you feel about the characters and the story you are telling, even indirectly. Here is an example of that from my own work, a novel I called *The Best Is Yet To Be:*

It was a beautiful day. The sun shone, and it was warm enough to go out without a coat. In the flower stalls along the Arno there were daffodils and lilies, and over the grass in the Boboli Gardens a faint, fresh green ran out as if it had been spilled there. The pines stood motionless against the blue sky, there was the sound of fountains, and, as if they had come out with the daffodils and the lilies, there were lovers on the paths everywhere.

The purpose of this descriptive passage is primarily to set the scene, but it also fulfills another important function of description, to create a mood. Description has other legitimate functions too. It helps the reader see a character more clearly—his background, his interests, his tastes, his past can be revealed in the way he has decorated his room and in the objects with which he surrounds himself.

Like any tool, it has to be used with discretion. Lengthy description can slow down the development of the plot. The reader rightly grows impatient with a writer who does not get on with his story.

It is necessary to remember that description must not become a digression that loses the forward thrust of the plot. It must always serve a specific purpose, and you should feel at all times that you know what this purpose is and that you are in control of it. If you find yourself writing at random, describing people or places without quite knowing where all of it is leading, as if you had fallen in love with your own words, it is perhaps best to stop and ask yourself what you are *not* doing.

It may be that instead of writing description, you should be writing a scene of action or of conversation. Keep in mind the rule of *Show, don't tell*. Let the story unfold and take place in front of the reader.

:seven:
The Necessary Scene

In the necessary scene the two contending forces meet in direct confrontation and one wins over the other. The lives of the characters are changed. Nothing will ever be quite the same again. If the conflict in your story is between two people, it is the principal character, the protagonist, who will be changed by whatever takes place. If the events revealed in your story have not changed him in some way, if he does not become a different person, your story will not be successful.

: 45 :

cannot have this climax take place outside the range
tory. If you are watching a play in which the suspense
builds until there is a murder, you will feel cheated if the
murder takes place offstage and you are merely told about it.
The emotional impact will be lost. The reader wants to be
shown, not told.

It is sometimes said among experienced writers that an
author always knows when he has come to the necessary
scene, because this is the scene he cannot write.

This paradox is an essential part of the nature of a story.
If, on the one hand, a writer feels that he is unable to write
the necessary scene because he is too inexperienced or hasn't
enough talent, he also knows that if the story is to be a success
he *must* write the necessary scene.

It is by learning to write the necessary scene that the
amateur or beginning writer makes the great leap forward
toward professional artistry.

Nevertheless, in many stories the necessary scene simply is
not there. There are ways to cheat, to get around writing this
scene. Some writers become so skillful at masking its absence
that their stories are published anyway. They are the stories
that leave us with a vague feeling of letdown, of having been
swindled along the way. They are the stories we soon forget.

One way to cheat is to fall back on a trick used in the
theater of ancient Greece. At its best, the theater in Greece
reached a very advanced stage. Much was done in the way
of elaborate costumes and stage settings and mechanical
devices for theatrical effects.

The Greeks contrived a simple way to help a writer avoid
having to write the necessary scene. Hidden behind a bank

of painted clouds was an enormous crane. When the action in a play became so involved and the relationships between the characters so confused that even the playwright could not bring things to some sort of satisfactory conclusion, he simply had one of the gods descend from Mount Olympus by means of the crane to straighten everything out.

This device became so well known that the words for it, in Latin, have passed into our language. When difficulties of a story are solved by the providential intervention of an outside force or person we refer to it as the *deus ex machina*, which means, literally, "the god from the machine."

Today the god from the machine is very often visible in the work of television or movie writers who are not very competent. For example, a wagon train of pioneers is going west. Suddenly they are surrounded by a band of hostile Indians. The pioneers form a circle with their wagons, hide the women and children inside, and defend themselves against the Indians with their rifles. Shouting war cries, the Indians gallop around the circle of wagons and shoot at the pioneers with bows and arrows. How can this story possibly end?

But wait! What is that sound? It is the sound of horses galloping! A bugle is blowing! Over the hill, banners flying, appears a regiment of soldiers of the United States Cavalry, just in time to save the beleaguered pioneers!

There, in the form of the cavalry, is the god from the machine, lowered from the clouds by the writer who couldn't figure out how to get his characters out of the trouble he had got them into in the first place.

Of course, the sound of the bugle blowing and of the horses galloping and the sight of the uniformed soldiers with their banners can be very exciting. It is a relief to know that the pioneers will be saved. Even the Indians will be able to retreat without loss when they see that they are outnumbered.

In real life such a confrontation would probably have had a different outcome. The battle would have gone on, and in the end one side would have won. Either the pioneers would have succeeded in driving the Indians away or the Indians would have defeated the pioneers.

That would have been a very different scene, much more difficult to write. It would have meant more character development, with the leaders of both forces drawn more clearly as they confronted each other in what, we now can see, was the necessary scene.

The reader of a story does want things to turn out right. Perhaps they won't, but the reader must be given hope that they could. Whatever happens, he wants the ending of the story to seem right. He doesn't want the problem of a story solved by a messenger arriving with a letter, or the hero receiving a legacy through a will. The ending of a story must seem to be the natural consequence of whatever deeds the characters have done.

Let us return to the Western story to illustrate this. The Western story is uniquely our own. It is often called the morality play of America. No matter who is in the story, or what takes place in the story, the plot is always the same. This plot is the conflict between good and evil, between the good guys and the bad guys. And because it is our morality play, it must always end in the same way. Good must triumph over evil. The good guy, or guys, must win.

In this example the necessary scene is handled better than it was in the previous example.

The villain, Hank Nogood, has come to Last Chance City to track down the marshal. Marshal Good once tracked down Hank Nogood's brother Oscar, who committed a murder, and he had Oscar Nogood tried and hanged. Now Hank Nogood is going to avenge his brother by killing Marshal Good.

The people of Last Chance City see Hank Nogood coming. Someone runs to warn Marshal Good, to tell him that he is in danger. But Marshal Good has no fear of any man, and he goes out to meet Hank Nogood, while everyone else runs to hide.

It is noon in Last Chance City. It is blistering hot under the sun. Main Street is dusty and deserted. There are no shadows anywhere, and there is no sound.

Slowly, deliberately, Hank Nogood and Marshal Good walk toward each other down the middle of the street. No one runs from cover to intervene. No god from the machine is lowered from the clouds to try to save the men from each other. When they get within shooting distance of each other, Hank Nogood suddenly draws his pistol. But Marshal Good is too fast for him. He pulls his gun and fires, wounding Hank Nogood in his shooting arm, forcing him to drop his pistol. Marshal Good takes him into custody, to be treated for his injury and booked for his intent to kill.

This scene is a classic example of the climax of our American morality play. Good and evil have met in direct conflict, and good has triumphed again.

Of course the conflict in a story is not always between good and evil. Even when it is, in stories other than Westerns, good does not necessarily triumph.

But whatever the outcome, the scene must be there. The reluctant writer will find that while it represents his greatest challenge, it also solves his problems. Once it is written, it will be easy to bring the story to an effective and believable end.

:eight:
The Storyteller's Tools

The tools of the storyteller are, quite simply, those of spelling, grammar, punctuation, and syntax. It must be said quite bluntly that without a working knowledge of these tools the writer of a story has very little chance of success.

To get an idea of how absolutely important it is, try to recall a favorite story of your own. While you were reading it, were you aware of the words? Were you conscious of how they were used? Did you notice whether they were spelled correctly? Did you check on the grammar and the punctuation to make sure that no mistakes were made?

Of course not. You enjoyed it.

The ultimate goal of any writer is to achieve such mastery of his tools that the reader will not be aware of them. The writing should not direct attention to itself, but instead should call up images or pictures in the mind of the reader.

This book has been written with a belief that the art of writing a story cannot be taught. However, the disciplines essential to that art can and must be learned. To illustrate this truth, with what is perhaps an exaggerated example, here is the transcript of an actual letter, written by a twelve-year-old girl from her home in the hill country of West Virginia, a part of that deprived area of our country known as Appalachia, to a visiting nurse who had come to see her:

> I an sorry I Didn't answer your letter Sonar. I was so glad to hear forn you. I an going to School every Day. Diana went last Friday to have her stitches taking out. the burn on my arn is Better Now I ben sick for a while. My mothe is going to the doctor Nonday. I an in the six grade this year. My teacher mane is nis smith. I an in the bed write you my dog is in the bed with me were did you moved to

The reader is immediately struck by the pathos of this letter. The young girl lives in an isolated area of great poverty. She has not had many of the opportunities that most of us take for granted, particularly in education.

But although she is untutored she does have a story to tell. She has that, indeed, whether she knows it or not. It is a story of the conflict between a people and their environment, and their triumph or defeat in the face of such hardships. Yet even if she could be made aware that she has a story of great interest to write, and even if she should want to write that story, she would have a hard time doing it, simply because she does not have a minimal control of her tools.

As a result, the moving story she has to tell would be incomprehensible to many people. Poignant as her letter is, if she tried to write it as a story, her mistakes in spelling, grammar, and punctuation, and her inability to compose a sentence would get between her and many readers and block their understanding of what her words might convey.

The result can be the same for anyone who tries to write a story. No matter how compelling that story may be, no matter how engrossing it is, it will not succeed if the reader's attention is diverted from the story to the flaws in the writing.

Grammar and spelling, punctuation and sentence structure are learned in school. In addition to these learned skills, a writer must acquire his own dictionary. It is the most precious possession he can have. He must train himself to use it on every occasion when he has the slightest doubt about the spelling or the meaning of a word.

Until you have mastered your craft, it is helpful to follow a worthy model. In reading a writer you admire, it is well to stop afterward, or even while reading, to analyze the writing to see how the writer achieved his effects.

A practice that many professional writers tried in the early years of their careers is one they learned from painters. In a museum one sometimes sees a student painter sitting at his easel in front of a picture he admires, carefully copying it. In this way he learns how the paint is applied, what strokes to take for what effect, how color is used.

A student writer can do the same thing. Simply open a book

to a page of a story you admire. Place it in front of you on a desk or a table. Then sit down with paper and pencil and copy that page of the story carefully, exactly as the author wrote it. There is hardly any better way to approach a mastery of the practical details of writing. In copying a page of writing one learns many important things. One learns how a sentence is formed for best effect. One learns something of what dictates the structure of a paragraph and determines the beginning of a new one. And one is also struck by the immense importance of punctuation. That is particularly true in the writing of conversation, where the commas, periods, question marks, and exclamation points enclosed by the quotation marks convey much of the meaning. In choosing pages of writing to copy, it is well to include some on which there is an abundance of dialogue.

You will be rewarded for your diligence in a way that can scarcely be described. A wonderful sense of freedom will come to you when you have mastered technical details. You will find, to your happy surprise, that you no longer have to think about them while writing.

Once you have learned the rules, you can even break them to achieve an effect. An important goal of the writer is to achieve such mastery of his tools that, like the reader, he can ignore them. Good writing must be free of flaws that might otherwise prevent the reader from receiving images, scenes, and sensations from the mind of the writer, much as he sees a picture on a television set without thinking of the complex mechanism behind it.

:nine:
Rewriting

It will surely seem like a contradiction to say now that when you begin to write a story, everything you have read so far in this book must be, for the time being, forgotten. In its original state a story is an untidy work. The material of a first draft can be misspelled, erased, added to, unpunctuated, unparagraphed if it comes out that way in the excitement and emotion of getting it down on paper. No writer with any self-respect would ever permit anyone to see this first draft anyway.

The process of writing the second draft is more deliberately thoughtful than the writing of the first draft, but it is gratifying in its own way. Now your conscious mind will come into play to review, with whatever perspective you can achieve about your own work, what you did when you were writing freely from your subconscious mind.

The first thing you may notice is that, more often than not, the beginning of the story is slow, or seems to take a long time to get off the ground. Very often the tension or conflict that forms the subject of the story is not there in the first pages. A great deal of the opening material of your first draft of a story may be merely an explanation of the characters and of the setting.

Again a trick can be used, one familiar to experienced writers. Turn to the top of page three of the first draft of your story and start reading there. You will be astonished to discover how often a story will begin at the top of page three of the first draft!

Here the characters may begin to speak for the first time. Here the conflict—which is so necessary to rouse the reader's interest—may be revealed. Here is where the action begins. Writers sometimes speak of the "hook" of a story. Since no one is required to read any story, it is necessary to hook a reader's interest at the outset so that he will want to continue. Often you will find that hook for your story at the top of page three of the first draft.

It would be a mistake, however, to discard those first two pages of the first draft. There may be material there that is necessary, or will become necessary, for a complete understanding of the story. The details of the descriptions or exposition can often be inserted into the story farther on—in

conversations between the characters, or as a character re-
members something that has happened before. A certain
amount of exposition is necessary, but often it is better used
later on in the story.

When you have determined where your story begins, then
you must examine the rest of it carefully to see whether all of
the necessary elements are there. Does the story have a middle and an end as well as a beginning? Does it build steadily
toward the climax? Is the necessary scene in the story, so
that the conflict is resolved in front of the reader?

This writing of the second draft of a story may be more
exciting than you might think. Here you can play around with
alternate ways to convey the same ideas, perhaps by turning
passages of what had been exposition into dialogue or scenes
between characters.

On the other hand, you may find in writing the second draft
of a story that there are passages of description or exposition
that you now want to cut out, in order to hasten the action of
the story. A curious thing about cutting in writing, or omit-
ting, as we noted earlier, is that very often the material left
out seems to remain in the story, in a way that is not easy to
explain. Most of us have an unconscious habit of repeating
ourselves, sometimes saying the same thing in different ways.
If some of this repetition is cut out, what is left seems even
more vivid or compelling by contrast. A good use of cutting
will often heighten the drama or suspense of a story.

When all of this has been done to the best of your ability,
then it is time to think of going on to the third and hopefully
final draft. Now you should have your dictionary at hand.
The story must be written out or typed again. There can be

no hasty compromise with absolute accuracy in the details of spelling, grammar, punctuation, and whatever knowledge you have of sentence structure and the forming of a paragraph.

Still, there must be no sense of discouragement as you near the end of writing a story. It is consoling to remember that no writer is ever completely satisfied with his work when he is finished with it, no matter how many years he may have been writing. Throughout the years, as a writer develops, he sees new possibilities ahead of him as a writer. To him, the story he hasn't written yet is always better than the one he has just finished. Perfection always eludes him. He never writes as well as he wishes he might.

Experienced writers learn to content themselves with the knowledge that they have made the greatest demand upon their ability of which they are capable at the moment. They have done the very best they can—nothing less will do.

When a writer sits down to write a story he is performing in a tradition that goes back to the beginning of history. It is almost possible to say that civilization began with the first writer, and recorded history is in itself a kind of story.

It is not necessary to be awed by this knowledge. Some people say that those who write stories are those who imagine they understand least about life and living. They write in an effort to understand. They are, in this theory, rather like mathematicians, putting figures down on a sheet of paper with the hope of solving a problem that baffles them.

For the writer of stories, life is that problem. On the sheet of paper in front of him he records what he sees and hears, and in the process arrives at a greater understanding of life.

Rewriting

One of our American writers, Thornton Wilder, has written a story called *The Woman of Andros*, which takes place on an island of ancient Greece. In this story a young man named Pamphilus, in a time of trouble for himself, walks out of his house and looks up at the sky and asks, "How does one live? What does one do first?"

All of us ask that question. All of us. We never stop asking that question. For, although there are millions of us, each of us is separate and new, and most of what we do, especially when we are young, we must do without benefit of the experience of other people, which might not apply to us.

It is well to remember that the great writer is usually one who writes about his subjects with love and compassion, not as a judge. A judge belongs in a court of law, not at a desk writing a story about people. If, as a writer, you are able to make the reader understand why your characters behave as they do, it may help him to understand himself better too, and the problems of life that confront him. If your story is successful, the reader may be entertained, or amused, or engaged in suspense or excitement, but he will be enriched by the experience of having read it, and his vision of life will be enlarged.

The way to learn to write is to write.

A journey of a thousand miles begins with a single step.

A story is written one word at a time.

Index

Index

2   3   4   5   75   74   73   72